Original title:
A Handbag for the Heart

Copyright © 2025 Creative Arts Management OÜ
All rights reserved.

Author: Nora Sinclair
ISBN HARDBACK: 978-1-80586-028-0
ISBN PAPERBACK: 978-1-80586-500-1

Handles of Hope

In a purse of dreams, I carry light,
A messy wallet that gives me a fright.
Coins roll and dance, in a vibrant spree,
They jingle my joy like a wild melody.

Lipstick treasures and crumbs of delight,
Lost the keys? Oh what a silly sight!
Yet in this chaos, I find my way,
Through pockets of laughter, come what may.

Clutched Memories

Snacks from last week, now a crunchy surprise,
Old receipts whisper of long-buried lies.
Each item a tale, uncurled with a grin,
My purse is a capsule where memories spin.

A gummy bear squished, a button long gone,
A mystery sock hiding, I carry them on.
With each shake and rattle, stories unfold,
Laughter erupts—my life's worth is gold.

The Purse of Persuasion

With a wink and a smile, I wield my charm,
This bag holds my secrets, my personal balm.
I reach for the snacks, charisma in hand,
Convinced all the world is at my command.

Buttoned and zipped with a playful flair,
It whispers sweet nothings while I stop and stare.
Pockets of magic, where mischief can dwell,
In my little satchel, I cast a good spell.

Heartstrings Tied with Ribbons

Checkered with laughter, this fabric of mine,
Ties memories neatly like ribbons that shine.
A sprinkle of chaos with style to spare,
I carry my heart, my treasures laid bare.

Ticklish and bright, odd nicknacks reside,
A tiny mirror sings of the fun that I hide.
With each little treasure, a giggle ignites,
My whimsical purse brings whimsical sights.

The Satchel of Sincerity

In a bag full of laughs, I keep my joy,
A lost sock and a rubber duck, oh what a ploy!
Lipstick and gum, a treasure trove near,
Every zipper's a secret, every pocket sincere.

A sandwich (crusts removed) hides next to the fluff,
An umbrella that's broken, we've had quite enough!
Receipts from last month? What a curious find,
This satchel of giggles, my heart intertwined.

Confetti from parties, a ticket or two,
A couple of love notes, scribbled just for you.
Balloons from the birthdays I may never reclaim,
In here lives my humor, forever the same.

So let's march through the day, with this bag at my side,
Trust in the contents, let laughter be our guide.
While hearts may be heavy, this satchel is light,
With each silly trinket, we'll soar to new heights.

Keepsakes in Containment

In a pouch of delight, my quirks find their space,
Leftover party hats and a rubber chicken's grace.
The remnants of snacks make a crunchy parade,
This whimsical hoard, I will never trade.

Peeking for lip balm, I find candy instead,
A fortune cookie slip, a sprightly thread.
Matching socks are in here, but wait… hold a sec,
I've only got one! What a fashionable wreck!

Nostalgia abounds with a dance party tape,
And a tiny old keychain that fell from my cape.
With each laugh concealed, and a slight, silly sigh,
These keepsakes contain laughter, they simply won't die.

So toss in a giggle, stuff in the cheer,
This vessel of whimsy brings joy ever near.
Who knew life's little bits could spark so much fun?
In this playful containment, our hearts will outrun.

Purses of Past and Present

Oh, the clutch I used to carry,
Filled with trinkets, quite so scary!
Lipstick, gum, and ancient keys,
Memories locked in fabric pleas.

Now my tote's a closet wide,
With snacks and dreams all piled inside.
A treasure map of what I hold,
A comical tale yet to be told.

The Tapestry of Yearnings

Stitched with laughter, sprinkled tears,
Each thread a wish that reappears.
Buttons clink like distant chimes,
Echoing the silliest of times.

Each pocket hides a sweet regret,
Or maybe just a snack I met.
A tapestry of want and whim,
A handbag dance on a playful limb!

Locks and Keys of the Heart

Where's the lock for my delight?
Perhaps it's in my purse tonight.
With shiny keys to laughter's door,
And memories I can't ignore.

Hiding gems from days gone by,
In this bag, emotions fly.
Unlocking joy with every peek,
Each quirky find makes my heart squeak.

Shelves of Sorrows and Joys

On a shelf, my purse sits proud,
With quirks that make my heart feel loud.
It holds both giggles and some sighs,
Treasures masked in disguise.

A place for candy, hopes, and dreams,
A jester's cap, or so it seems.
Each glance inside brings forth a cheer,
For every story's worth a beer!

Love's Little Pouch

In the depths of my purse, a surprise,
Old receipts and a pair of tight ties.
A gum wrapper, a crumpled note,
Who knew love came stuffed in this tote?

Lip gloss smudged like a tender kiss,
Forgetful moments, can't let those miss.
Oh, the chaos that love can bring,
Tucked within this bag, it's the little things.

Baggage of Belonging

This grumpy old bag, it knows my quirks,
    From date night blunders to coffee perks.
    It holds my secrets, both big and small,
    Even a snack for when hunger calls.

With broken zippers and a missing strap,
    It's like a relationship—just a bit of a trap.
    Yet, it carries memories in all its creases,
    A quirky companion, never it ceases.

Heirloom of Heartstrings

Passed down from grandma, a relic of cheer,
   It's stained with love, both laughter and tear.
   Filled with odd knickknacks, each has a tale,
  Just like my heart's journey, a curious trail.

  This pouch says it all, in its cluttered way,
  A button from first love, it's here to stay.
    Tucked in a pocket, warmth it brings,
An heirloom crafted with heart's own strings.

The Clasp of Connection

Locked up inside, my feelings do jig,
   Like a trapped squirrel in a cutesy fig.
  The clasp of my bag, it knows all my woes,
   And the goofy moments nobody knows.

Tied tight with laughter, or maybe some tears,
It guards tales of love, and forgotten years.
  Not the perfect fit, but a snug little sight,
Where my heart shares its giggles, both day and night.

Heartstrings and Leather

In a purse so fine, I feel my heart,
It carries my dreams, plays a vital part.
Lipstick and laughter, tucked away tight,
A zippered secret, that sparkles so bright.

With each little change, emotions align,
A wallet of wishes, all faithfully mine.
Coins for my thoughts, clinks of delight,
In the world of the bags, I twirl with insight.

Clutches of Sentiment

Oh, the clutches I hold, they whisper and tease,
Filled with my stories, like a warm summer breeze.
With patterns so wild, and colors so bold,
Each grab is a giggle, a treasure to hold.

I clutch with both hands, as joy comes alive,
In pockets of memories, our laughter will thrive.
Beneath the shine, a soft heart will dwell,
Each trip to the shops, a whimsical spell.

The Satchel of Longing

In my satchel so spacious, I dream and I sigh,
A map of my wishes, laid out in the sky.
Wrapped in soft fabric, it holds all my cheer,
A stylish companion, always near.

With pockets aplenty, it treasures my woes,
Each trinket I find, like petals on prose.
It carries my giggles, my sighs, and my schemes,
A recipe of longing, forever it beams.

Treasure Trove of Tenderness

Inside my trove, there's laughter and whim,
A beacon of warmth, my heart on a limb.
With each chocolate token, my love finds a place,
It's soft, it's delightful, with charm and with grace.

Buttons and doodads, a whimsical stash,
Help me remember, in a cluttered dash.
Heartfelt adventures, all neatly ensconce,
In pockets of joy, my sentiments prance.

A Bag of Yearnings

In a bag stuffed with dreams, I dive,
Seeking treasures where wishes thrive.
Lipstick and laughter, all jumbled and neat,
A sparkling ensemble, a whimsical feat.

With each zip and unzip, my heart does a flip,
Chasing rainbows with a sarcastic quip.
Who needs a map when I have this flair?
A purse full of giggles, with room to spare!

The Enigma of Emotions

What's hidden away in this velvet embrace?
A riddle of feelings, hard to trace.
Tissues for tears and snacks for delight,
Mood swings on a rollercoaster, hold on tight!

The joy of a find, or a key to the past,
With each little trinket, I'm spellbound, aghast.
Who knew a clasp could hold so much fate?
This puzzle of feelings, is it love or just bait?

Timeless Transformations

From clutch to tote, my moods oscillate,
Changing with moments, oh, isn't it great?
One day I'm glitzy, the next I'm laid-back,
With a wink to the world, and a quirk in my pack.

In a flash, I'm a princess or a rockstar in jeans,
Every outfit a canvas, and my handbag's the queen.
Swapping my charms like a game of charades,
Transformative magic, oh, the escapades!

Handcrafted Hopes

Stitched with desires and dreams slightly askew,
My bag tells a story—some old, some new.
Buttons of laughter, pockets of cheer,
Each little compartment holds something dear.

Crafted with care, its seams hold my fate,
Collecting the absurd, isn't life great?
With a wink and a nod, I smile at the absurd,
My bag's full of hopes, and oh, how they stirred!

Carried Emotions

Inside my bag, I stash my woes,
A crumpled love note that nobody knows.
Old receipts whisper of dates gone wrong,
Yet I carry on, humming my song.

Lipstick and laughter, all piled high,
A mirror reflects a bright, silly sigh.
I jingle my keys, unlocking the fun,
With a zip and a snap, my heart's on the run!

The Poetry of Possessions

With every trinket tucked away tight,
A glittering story, a small delight.
An old candy wrapper, a pen that won't write,
My bag's a poem, both awkward and bright.

There's a sweater of yarn I almost forgot,
Dancing with memories and tangled thought.
Each charm has a tale, some goofy, some sweet,
In the depths of my bag, life's chaos is neat!

Love's Woven Threads

Threads of affection, tangled and bold,
A scarf from the past, a story retold.
With buttons of laughter, and zippers of cheer,
My hand carries warmth, drawing you near.

Each stitch holds a giggle, a tear if you peek,
My heart keeps expanding, but never too sleek.
I zip up my feelings all snug in their place,
As I waltz through the world, with style and grace.

Sewn-Up Sorrows

What's that lurking, a ghost of old pain?
Tucked in the corner, it's hard to explain.
A project half-finished, its threads start to fray,
 Yet I carry it still, in a humorous way.

A needle of laughter stitches me whole,
As I sift through the darkness, searching for soul.
With pockets of giggles, and sorrows aflight,
 I strut down the street, my future is bright!

Clutching Dreams

In the depths of my tote, they gleam,
Sparkles of wishes knit in a seam.
Lipstick and hopes, all swirled together,
I'm fishing for magic, in any weather.

Tangled in threads of a whimsical plan,
Carried in style like no other can.
With my bag full of jest and secrets untold,
I strut through the world, feeling bold.

Filling Spaces with Meaning

Nibbles of joy in a pocket, you see,
Packed tight with giggles, just like me.
Bangs in the zipper, and crumbs in the fold,
Memories scattered like painted gold.

A dance of madness, colors collide,
My trusty little friend, always by my side.
Each trinket and token, a story to share,
Life's fluffy confetti, held with care.

The Fabric of Connection

Stitching together a comical tale,
Threads of friendship, never stale.
Looks exchanged and laughter is spun,
Each fabric patch tells how we've fun.

Fashion faux pas and style so quirky,
Comments are made, slightly jerky.
Yet in this patchwork, love we find,
Stitched with humor, it's all aligned.

Holding on to Hope

In this little pouch lies my dream,
Woven with laughter, not always a theme.
It jingles and clinks, style full of glee,
Treasures unfurling, oh look! There's me!

Each button, each knot, a giggle inside,
Packed with mischief, in colors I hide.
I sift through the chaos, my heart's delight,
Holding on tightly, I'm ready to fight.

Whispers in the Pocket

In a pocket deep and wide,
Secrets whisper, they can't hide.
Change from laughter, crumbs of cheer,
A strange mine where hopes appear.

Bags hold dreams and snacks galore,
But what's that lump? Oh, what's in store?
A half-eaten muffin? Or was it a shoe?
What's funny is, I still love you!

Secrets Stitched in Time

Each stitch hides tales of yesteryear,
A button fails, yet we still cheer.
Who needs style when you've got flair?
This odd-shaped bag's beyond compare.

Tangled threads and stories fold,
With every zipper, they unfold.
What's that smell? Is it old cheese?
Or maybe just my heart's unease?

The Carryall of Emotions

In this tote, emotions blend,
Laughter's light, but tears descend.
My heart's a mix of joy and strife,
All packed together, much like life.

Sometimes it tips, spills out a song,
A slice of life that feels so wrong.
Oh look, my smile turned into a frown,
Who knew feelings weighed this much down?

Tattered Dreams

Inside this bag, dreams worn and torn,
Some days bright, others forlorn.
But isn't it fun to chase a whim?
Even with edges frayed and dim?

Collecting bits like scavenger hunts,
A sock, a pebble, oh, what fun!
A jumbled mess, but don't you see?
This chaos is just so very free!

Tender Lullabies

My handbag hums a gentle tune,
Of chocolate bars and spoons at noon.
It's a concert of crinkled dreams,
Where silly giggles burst at seams.

What else is lurking, who can tell?
A duster, a sock? Oh, do ring the bell!
Grab a tune, or maybe a hat,
This bag's a friend, and oh, how I chat!

Emotionally Tailored

In a patchwork of feelings, I giggle and sway,
Each stitch is a memory, come what may.
Zippers for secrets, buttons for dreams,
My bag holds my laughter, or so it seems.

Fabric of whims, it's snug and it's tight,
Quirky and vibrant, it's pure delight.
With pockets for mishaps and seams for my woes,
I carry my chaos wherever it goes.

A Caress in Every Compartment

There's a shimmer of joy tucked under the flap,
Compartment of cuddles, beneath my knee wrap.
With a twinkle of glitter and a puff of the charm,
It hugs all my feels; it keeps me from harm.

A pencil for daydreams, a mirror for smiles,
I rummage for giggles and stay for a while.
Each nook filled with quirks, with a pinch of surprise,
It's my little treasure, where joy multiplies.

Pockets Full of Poetry

In the depths of my carry-all, verses collide,
With phrases that bounce like a joyride.
There's a sonnet for snacks, a rhyme for a trip,
Words overflowing like candy from a lip.

I pull out a stanza as I walk down the street,
With a chorus of chuckles, life feels complete.
It's a bag full of laughter, a whimsy parade,
Each pocket a poem, ready to trade.

The Weight of Wishes

Oh, the burden of dreams in this stylish old thing,
With wishes stacked high like a circus ring.
The scales tipped by hopes I carelessly toss,
Like candy in pockets, I'll carry the loss.

Sheepishly weighted with giggles and sighs,
A hope falls out when it comes as a surprise.
The charm of my handbag keeps wishes in flow,
Slinging joy like confetti, just watch it glow!

Embrace in Every Fold

In pockets deep, where secrets hide,
A crumpled note, a love inside.
With lipstick wars and crumbs galore,
A treasure map of tales in store.

Keys jingle like a happy tune,
A wallet's laugh beneath the moon.
Each zipper tells a funny tale,
Of adventure's charm that cannot fail.

Oh, wristlets dance with dreamy flair,
They hold the woes, but knit the care.
With every fold, a joke unfolds,
In fabric stitched with stories bold.

So hold it tight, your heart's delight,
In playful pouches, all feels right.
Laughter echoes in each design,
A loving heart, forever mine.

Love's Luggage

A suitcase bright, it springs with cheer,
Packed with giggles, never fear.
Socks and dreams in disarray,
This silly baggage leads the way.

Oh, travel tips in scattered notes,
A map of love in crinkled coats.
Each pair of shoes, a dancing pair,
Their silly steps light up the air.

Unwanted fluff from passions passed,
Yet none can rival memories amassed.
With every zip, a sigh of bliss,
This funny haul, we won't dismiss.

So grab your bags, let's hit the road,
With laughter's weight, we'll share the load.
For on this journey, never part,
Let's chase the sun, and pack the heart.

Fashioning a Safe Haven

In pouches soft, where hopes reside,
A quirky charm, our hearts confide.
With buttons bright and threads that twirl,
This fabric holds our goofy whirl.

A flap of joy, a pocket wide,
Where dainty dreams and giggles hide.
With every press, a funny thought,
In this retreat, all's dearly bought.

Stitched with care, a cozy nook,
With doodles drawn in every book.
The world outside may spin and race,
But here within, we find our place.

So wear it proud, this playful shell,
A sanctuary where we dwell.
In vibrant shades of laughter's hue,
Our favorite spot, just me and you.

The Burden of Cherished Relics

Old receipts hold memories tight,
Of pizza nights and laughter bright.
A stray button, lost but not alone,
This quirky crew, our comfort zone.

A coffee stain, a lipstick smudge,
Tales of romance that won't budge.
Each little trinket speaks to me,
In delightful chaos, hearts run free.

But oh, the weight of past's embrace,
Fashion's laugh in tangled space.
These relics funny, silly, dear,
In every crease, a story's near.

So lift it high, this lovely load,
With every step, let laughter explode.
In all the mess, we find the art,
For joy is woven from the heart.

Adornments of Affection

With pockets deep and colors bright,
A heart that carries laughter light.
Each trinket says, 'Oh, look at me!'
A joy parade, come dance with glee.

Beneath the seams, a secret stash,
Of whispered dreams and a silly laugh.
A zipper that catches love on the way,
And reminds us to play everyday.

From sparkly pins to feathered charms,
Each little gift, a hug that warms.
Daydreams tucked in the smallest nook,
A treasure chest, come take a look!

So when you roam with flair and twist,
Remember each purse holds a sweet tryst.
With every snap, a smile set free,
Adornments of joy for you and me.

Handcrafted Hopes

In corners where oddities blend,
A purse of dreams, where wishes send.
With every stitch, a tale is spun,
A clumsy dance that's bound to run.

The handles sway like comedy,
With mishaps and giggles, a symphony.
Laughter spills from a quirky clasp,
A heartfelt joy you cannot grasp.

Each pocket tells a joke or two,
Of mishaps and blunders we often do.
With a wink and nod, here's what we share,
Handcrafted hopes, beyond compare.

So pack your dreams and frolic wide,
With a charming bag, you'll soon abide.
In every crack, a smile does gleam,
Your hopes all cradled in a zany dream.

A Satchel of Silent Wishes

In the shadows where thoughts conspire,
A bag that holds both heart and fire.
With zippers that giggle and buttons that tease,
A satchel stirs only joyful breeze.

Tucked away, the dreams take flight,
Whispers of love disguised in light.
Hidden treasures that bounce and sway,
Turn frowns to laughter, come what may.

From scratchy notes to a sweet surprise,
It holds the glimmers in our eyes.
In every fold, a chuckle survives,
A whimsical charm that truly thrives.

So swing it round and show some flair,
In a satchel of wishes, we find our care.
For laughter's the fabric that threads us tight,
And dreams are the pockets, shining bright.

Bolts of Passion

In the chaos of color, joy ignites,
A purse of zeal that sparks delights.
With seams that pop and linings that sing,
Bolts of passion take to wing.

Each snap a giggle, every clasp a cheer,
Filled to the brim with hopes and fear.
A symphony of style, both silly and sweet,
With every touch, makes life complete.

So pack it full with smiles galore,
In this wild adventure, you'll find much more.
From spangles to jokes, life's grand array,
Bolts of passion light up the day.

So grab your bag, it's time to roam,
For in its embrace, we find our home.
With laughter as fuel, hearts take the lead,
In this playful journey, we all take heed.

Emotions in Every Stitch

In this little purse, secrets swing,
Joy and chaos, a jumbled bling.
Laughter bounces from side to side,
As worries hide where they won't confide.

Zippers giggle when opened wide,
Guarding grumbles we like to hide.
Every thread a tale that's spun,
Heartfelt mischief—who could outrun?

Pockets hold a snack or two,
For midnight cravings that ensue.
A compact cradle for silly sights,
Happiness packed in colorful bites.

So when you see this lovely chest,
Remember it carries your funny quest.
With every squeeze, there's laughter's art,
Emotions woven, stitched from the heart.

Charming Pockets of Emotion

In a pocket, a grumpy cat sleeps,
Next door, a dancing sock leaps.
A smile hides behind the clasp,
While a hairpin dreams, hoping to grasp.

Buttons squabble, lost in flair,
Each tells tales beyond compare.
A charm for giggles, big and small,
Whispering memories, catch them all.

A smudge of lipstick, bright and bold,
Remnants of laughter that never gets old.
Like confetti thrown in a wild place,
Charming pockets hide joy's embrace.

So open it wide, don't be shy,
Seek the silliness tucked nearby.
With every search, laughter appears,
Charming pockets bursting with cheers!

Whispers in Soft Leather

The whispers of dreams are stitched up tight,
With dreams of mischief that take flight.
Each crease and curve tells a joke,
A dapper tale just waiting to poke.

Soft leather laughs, with a wink and a nod,
Hiding treasures with an "Oh, my God!"
Tissues for giggles and dreams of cake,
All packed up, make no mistake.

Confessions of love tucked within folds,
A tiny umbrella for when it scolds.
With every snap signals a cheer,
Whispers of laughter always near.

So let it embrace, let it sway,
In the heart's softest, silliest way.
It carries not just things, you see,
But all the smiles that set us free.

The Carrying Case of Dreams

This playful pouch carries wishes galore,
Far beyond things it held before.
Tiny rainbows tucked inside,
With giggles waiting for a ride.

A coin or two for a silly song,
Hopes that somehow, nothing feels wrong.
Crayons of laughter and bits of fun,
Whirling around like a zany run.

With bows and tags that can't be found,
Plus whimsy that bounces all around.
It lifts the spirit, oh so bright,
A case of dreams, igniting the night.

So grab it quick, give it a squeeze,
Feel the joy dance in the breeze.
With every chaotic hop and skip,
This friendly case won't let dreams slip!

The Satchel of Sentiments

In a bag stitched with glee,
Lies the love note from me.
With a pen that won't run,
I'll write jokes just for fun.

A pocket for bits of delight,
Hiding snacks out of sight.
Each zipper, a giggle or two,
When I pull out my shoe!

With glitter and sparkles inside,
It's the place where I hide.
A secret, a chuckle, a tear,
This satchel brings laughter, my dear.

From trinkets to laughter, all snug,
One day I'll find a big bug.
But for now it's pure cheer,
This satchel, oh dear, oh dear!

Treasure Trove of Thoughts

Diving deep in this chest,
Where my dreams love to rest.
With postcards stuck from afar,
And a broken guitar.

A trinket from twelve, don't you see?
Mom's earrings hang free.
Each thought wrapped in a bow,
Have you seen my pet crow?

Lollipops, laughter, and more,
Hidden secrets galore!
A map leading to candy,
In this trove, oh so handy.

With each rummage and find,
I embrace what's behind.
A treasure hunt, oh so light,
Where silliness takes flight.

Sketches in Stitchwork

In threads of bright colors, they dance,
Each pattern whispers a chance.
Smiles sewn with a loop and a twist,
In this fabric, none can resist.

There's a doodle of a cat,
And beside it, my old hat.
This canvas holds laughter and cheer,
A patchwork of joy, my dear.

With each stitch, memories pop,
A quilt with giggles, no stop.
From clumsy hugs to silly pranks,
Life's stitched up in colorful ranks.

So let the thread twirl and spin,
For in this blanket, we'll win.
A masterpiece of friendship so bright,
Sewn with love, pure delight!

The Memory Keeper

In this box of wonder, I keep,
The secrets I vowed, I wouldn't leak.
Old tickets and notes abound,
Where laughter and stories are found.

A memory of pizza on the floor,
The day we forgot to lock the door.
With every clink of this jar,
Comes a moment, a bizarre memoir.

Sticky notes, oh what a sight,
Reminders of wild, sleepless nights.
Each keepsake wrapped with a chuckle,
A bubble of joy, how we snuggle.

So here's to the tales that we write,
In this keeper of memories, so light.
From silly to sweet, they cling tight,
Crafting our lives, a pure delight!

Love Knots and Stitches

In the purse of affection, I find,
A knot that binds us, oh so blind.
Stitches of laughter, tears they mend,
My quirky soulmate, my best friend.

Lipstick and dreams, all tossed inside,
Keys to our laughter, nowhere to hide.
Searching for pennies, I find a sock,
Woven with love, it's a ticking clock.

Amidst the tangle, I pull out a note,
Whispers of joy that keep us afloat.
A thread of quirk in this fabric so fine,
Each twist and turn, your hand in mine.

With every zipper that jangles with glee,
Another surprise stares back at me.
Like a magician's hat, it yields so much,
In this jumble of love, I'm always in touch.

Valuables of the Heart

In my bag, secrets and lies,
Treasures hidden from prying eyes.
Chocolate wrappers and old receipts,
Funny reminders of our heartbeats.

A broken toy, a sparkly ring,
Each little item makes my heart sing.
Notes scribbled wildly, in haste, in glee,
Like our own chaos, wild and free.

Can't find my phone, it's swallowed whole,
Yet it's all part of our playful role.
Doodles of wishes, plans in a mess,
Our quirky adventure, I must confess.

Toss in some laughter, squeeze in a kiss,
Amidst all the clutter, I find my bliss.
Each item a journey, each zip a delight,
In this arsenal of love, we're perfectly tight.

The Bundle of Belongings

Tangled up treasures, what a sight,
Each little piece tells a story bright.
A floral scarf, a ticket stub,
Echoes of laughter, a joyous hub.

Among the chaos, I find my dreams,
In crumpled corners, joy always beams.
A half-eaten snack, some mismatched socks,
Feeling rich with our quirky flocks.

Every layer unravels a grin,
What's lost in there is where we begin.
Stuffed with hopes and a joke or two,
This bundle of joy, I share with you.

Through zippers and pockets, love unfolds,
Cardboard memories, glittering golds.
In the jumble that is our delight,
We find happiness tucked in tight.

Carrying the Weight of Love

Weight of affection, oh, what a load,
Each item a memory on this strange road.
Balloons from parties, a rubber duck,
In the heart of my bag, I'm out of luck.

Each clanging key unlocks some glee,
A trinket that tells our history.
The weight of the world, but it's not all bad,
It's filled with the moments that make us glad.

Cracks in the fabric, a sign of wear,
But with every tear, I see how we care.
A shopping list filled with dreams, oh my,
This playful burden makes spirits fly.

So here's to the baggage we both shall share,
From mismatched socks to whispers in the air.
Each silly item, a piece of our story,
With every new laugh, we bask in the glory.

Fabrics of Feeling

Silk of laughter wraps around,
Threads of joy in every sound.
Velvet whispers hold a secret,
Cotton dreams that dare to peek.

Zippers mark the silly sighs,
Buttons hide the little lies.
Pockets stitched with love and fun,
Quilts of hope when day is done.

Chiffon clouds and taffeta tears,
Stitched in love to quiet fears.
Patchwork smiles and frayed old seams,
Fabrications made of dreams.

Gingham checkers, polka dots,
Stitching laughter in warm spots.
Every fiber tells a tale,
Of each trip, and every trail.

Adornments of Affection

Beads of giggles strung with care,
Ribbons flying through the air.
Charms that jingle, hearts that race,
Glittering with a playful grace.

Brooch of mischief holds a grin,
Pin it on, let laughter spin.
Earrings shaped like joyful sparks,
Dancing shadows in the parks.

Necklaces of whimsy twine,
Filling spaces, oh so fine.
Bracelets clasped with silly flair,
Happiness blooms everywhere.

Sashes tied with love's embrace,
Fringe of fun in every place.
Each adornment, light as air,
Gifts of giggles everywhere!

The Cradle of Contemplation

In a nook of thoughts so deep,
Dreams lay wrapped, soft and cheap.
A sleepy pouch to hold the views,
Where silly musings softly snooze.

Fringe of fancies, braided zeal,
Touch these threads, let feelings heal.
Old receipts of laughter kept,
Worn-out tales that once were wept.

Zany drawings pinned on high,
Chasing echoes, making shy.
Corner pieces of desire,
Fueling sparks that never tire.

A cradle made of thought and light,
Brewing joy both day and night.
In this space, embrace the quirks,
To find delight in playful works.

Pockets Full of Stars

My pockets bulge with twinkling dreams,
Whispers of joy and silly schemes.
Nights of laughter tucked away,
Cosmic giggles in a fray.

Stardust spills from every seam,
Dancing shadows in a gleam.
Catching wishes, throwing them wide,
Shooting stars in laughter's tide.

Zodiac charms and playful quirk,
Celestial smiles in every work.
Each pocket hides a world so bright,
Filled with wonder, pure delight.

Reach in deep, feel the glow,
Silly stories start to flow.
With every star, a giggle far,
Treasures found, like moons ajar.

Compartments of Courage

In pockets deep, my secrets rest,
Each zipper's grin, a playful jest.
With lint and love, it's well adorned,
Inside this bag, my dreams are born.

Loose change giggles, a crumpled note,
In a world of fluff, my hopes float.
Keys to laughter, a ticket to cheer,
Who knew courage could fit in here?

With every glance, it winks at me,
A jester's heart, daring to be free.
Adventures hide in each fold and seam,
This quirky pouch holds all my dreams.

So here's to courage, in each little clasp,
From fashion faux pas to quirky grasp.
With a twirl and swish, I strut with pride,
In this colorful bag, my dreams can't hide.

A Purse Full of Whimsy

A purse full of giggles, a sprinkle of glee,
Contains a compass, oh, just for me.
With candies and confetti, it jingles delight,
This magical satchel beams bright through the night.

A tiny umbrella, for raindrops of fun,
It wraps me in smiles when the day's begun.
With pockets of mischief and zippers of joy,
It holds all my dreams, like a playful toy.

With each flap's flutter, whimsical sights,
A kaleidoscope of colors, pure delights.
In this little wonder, my heart sings aloud,
For every adventure, my purse is proud.

So twirl and dance with this whimsical bag,
It's a treasure chest, never feels ragged.
In laughter and light, it shines like a star,
A purse full of whimsy is never bizarre.

The Silhouette of Solace

In shadows soft, my comfort's found,
A silhouette whispers, no need to astound.
With soft edges and curves, it hugs with flair,
A faithful companion, always there.

Each clasp a secret, each strap a smile,
While I wander through life, it goes every mile.
In moments of chaos, it stays by my side,
With mishaps and giggles, in laughter we glide.

Its fabric holds stories, stitched with grace,
In this gentle outline, I find my place.
A tender embrace in a bustling world,
A sanctuary soft, as dreams unfurled.

So here's to the forms that comfort the heart,
In whimsical shapes, where joy takes part.
With each passing moment, let's embrace the art,
For in its design, we never depart.

Heartfelt Designs

Crafted with love, each stitch a delight,
These vibrant patterns make my world bright.
With pockets for laughter and a zipper for dreams,
This playful masterpiece bursts at the seams.

The fabric of friendship, woven with care,
A dash of whimsy is hidden somewhere.
With every flap and fold, it sings a tune,
All my bright hopes dance beneath the moon.

From polka dots to stripes, a tapestry flows,
With colors like rainbows, my spirit it knows.
Each heartfelt design spins tales of cheer,
Encasing my passions, it's art, oh so dear.

So twine your dreams in this fabric divine,
Celebrate whimsy, let your heart shine.
For every creation that brings laughs and fun,
Is a heartfelt design where joy has begun.

Fashioned from Love's Fabric

In a world of zippers and threads,
I stitched my heart with silly beads.
With pockets full of joy and dread,
I carry dreams and quirky needs.

Buttons shaped like silly faces,
They wink and nod when folks walk by.
Each patch tells tales of silly places,
Where laughter echoes, oh so high.

Straps that hold the weight of glee,
With every bounce, my heart's alive.
This bag of quirks is part of me,
A playful ride, oh how I thrive!

So if you see me with this style,
Just know my heart is tucked inside.
A quirky bag that makes me smile,
In fashion's fun, I happily glide.

Herein Lies My Soul's Embrace

Within this bag, emotions swirl,
Like gumdrops tossed in a wild race.
With lipstick swirls and curls unfurl,
My spirit twirls in a warm embrace.

Laughter bounces off the sides,
With pocket mirrors reflecting fun.
From the heavens, joy abides,
As secrets dance in the sun.

Inside, a playlist of silly tunes,
That hum along with my heartbeat.
All my fears fly like balloons,
In this cozy, charming seat.

So come and peek inside my prize,
You'll find delight, a surprise or two.
A space where happiness never dies,
Wrapped snugly in my dreams for you.

Stitching Memories Together

With needle and thread, I craft my days,
Each stitch a laugh, each flap a cheer.
These moments bind in colorful ways,
Memories tucked away, forever near.

Sugar packets and love notes too,
Dance among the whims of fate.
They giggle and wink, a joyful crew,
In this pouch that I celebrate.

Every pocket's a tale to be spun,
Of mischief, joy, and a little strife.
With quirky charms, my heart is won,
This playful bag holds my vibrant life.

So as I wander, clutching tight,
Know every giggle finds a home.
In the fabric of love, I take flight,
United in laughter, I freely roam.

Beneath the Clasp of Affection

Under the clasp of cheeky bliss,
My heart's tucked away, safe and sound.
With each open flap, there's a kiss,
Of whimsy and laughter profound.

Inside, a treasure of light and jokes,
A sprinkle of glitter, spry and bright.
With folds that hold the giggling folks,
In this pouch, the world feels right.

So zip it up tight, hold it dear,
This whimsical bag, a delight to see.
It carries the magic of friendship near,
And all the silliness shared with me.

So let's dance with glee, every day,
With this joyful pouch, we'll take a stand.
In laughter and love, let's play,
Under the clasp, we hand in hand.

Lining the Corners of Desire

I found a treasure, quite absurd,
In a bag of hues, none unheard.
Lipsticks dancing, keys in a twirl,
A snack for later, oh what a whirl!

Hopes and wishes, stuffed with glee,
A crumpled receipt, a mystery!
Mismatched buttons, a love note stuck,
In the depths of this whimsical luck!

A lost earring, does it still shine?
Or is it waiting, a drink or nine?
A wallet giggles, its secret game,
In the corners where desires claim!

So rummage away, take a long dive,
In pockets and seams, that's where we thrive!
Laugh out loud at what you find,
In the corners where laughter unwinds!

Pocketful of Dreams

A pocket of dreams, oh what a scene,
Filled with all things cozy and keen.
Loose change whispering tales untold,
In a world of wishes, bright and bold.

A wrinkled map, to nowhere in sight,
Chased by a cat that's dreaming in night.
Chocolate wrappers, a fleeting kiss,
Life's little treasures, filled with bliss!

Notes from friends, penned with delight,
They laugh and giggle under moonlight.
An umbrella for two, you, me, and more,
The jingling coins dance on the floor!

So reach inside, let the dreams unfurl,
In this pocket of magic, where giggles swirl!
Life's little wonders, tucked away tight,
In the pocket of dreams, everything feels right!

Enchanted Carriers of Sentiment

These enchanted carriers, oh what a sight,
They hold our laughter, our spark, our light.
Buttons of memories, sewn in with care,
Twirling in sunset, a whimsical affair!

A polka dot scarf, a tale from the past,
Through tangled adventures, it's quite a blast!
With each little pocket, a giggle unfolds,
Bringing to life, the stories it holds!

The charm of a mirror, reflecting the fun,
Sparks in the eyes of everyone!
A forgotten snack brings joy uncontained,
In this world of chaos, where laughter remained!

So cherish these carriers, full of delight,
They cradle our secrets, so lovely and bright!
In this enchanted journey, let's laugh and partake,
For these carriers of sentiment, we joyfully make!

The Zippered Realm of Reminiscence

Enter the realm, zip it up tight,
Memories flutter, a whimsical flight.
Leftover popcorn, from last week's show,
In this wild kingdom, it's all aglow!

Lost laughter echoes under old seams,
Like a visit from the past in our dreams.
A funky sticker, a badge of pride,
In this zippered realm, treasures collide!

A receipt from dinner, where we dined like stars,
In a galaxy of giggles, and funny memoirs.
An old photo tucked, a wild hairdo,
Bringing back joys that were once so true!

The zipper sings stories in playful release,
In this realm where the heart finds peace.
So let's laugh together, as we rummage through,
In this forever space, where dreams come true!

Hidden Hues of Affection

In a pocket filled with mismatched dreams,
Lies a lipstick pink, or so it seems.
A crumpled note, a chocolate bar,
All tucked away like treasures bizarre.

With every zip, a giggle escapes,
Countless secrets in fancy shapes.
A wallet that tells tales very bold,
Of mishaps, laughter, and friendships gold.

In the depths of this quirky space,
There's always room for a cheeky trace.
A pair of sunglasses, slightly askew,
Reflecting moments utterly true.

Hidden hues hide the love we share,
Wrapped in fabric, with utmost care.
Each snippet whispers soft and sweet,
Tales of affection, a joyful treat.

Threads Woven from Desire

Stitch by stitch, desires unfold,
In a bag made of wishes, bright and bold.
Here's a thread pulled from a wild night,
With a laugh that still feels just right.

A keychain shaped like a winking cat,
Reminds me of where our love sat.
Tangled yarn of dreams and schemes,
All in the fabric of silly themes.

Buttons from shirts that never did fit,
Add charm to the chaos; every bit.
A fluffy pom-pom bounces with glee,
As I stroll down nostalgia's spree.

From pockets deep, the stories flow,
In a woven sac where good vibes grow.
Each thread holds a laugh, a little cheer,
A tapestry bright that brings you near.

Inflight of the Hearts

Packed with snacks for a jolly ride,
This charming handbag's a whimsical guide.
A ticket stub from the dance we missed,
Flies with the fluff that can't be dismissed.

Lip balm whispers 'let's never land!'
While quirky stickers await your hand.
A tiny UFO, from a cosmic spree,
Hitches a ride—oh, what a spree!

Bottled giggles in crimson hues,
Fly high with all the happy news.
A plush version of a heart's delight,
Spinning stories through day and night.

Inflight, we drift with heads in the clouds,
With dreams that feel both big and proud.
Each little trinket, a joke or two,
Reflects the journey I made with you.

The Tapestry of Longing

In this stitched tapestry of whimsy bright,
Lie band-aids for woes, as love takes flight.
A patchwork of laughter, some threads of doubt,
Where silly moments weave the heart about.

A sprinkle of glitter, a dash of flair,
This fabric holds secrets, each stitch laid bare.
A pocket of wishes, the oddest charms,
Wrapped snugly tight that keep us warm.

With dice from a game that never was played,
And buttons of laughter in colors displayed.
Every layer whispers tales of delight,
Like a cozy hug at the fall of night.

The tapestry tells of hope and cheer,
Of dreams chased down through every year.
In the quilt of our journey, love won't depart,
Every thread spun from the fabric of heart.

Threads of Treasured Moments

In my bag, a mystery hides,
Chocolates and a cat that abides.
Old receipts, a map from last year,
My wallet screams, "Please, draw near!"

Crumpled dreams and candy wrappers,
Laughter echoing, endless clappers.
A lipstick tint, now quite the mess,
Each item whispers, "I confess!"

Tiny notes from friends so dear,
Every crinkle tells a cheer.
Little treasures stacked in piles,
Each brings me back to carefree smiles.

So I zip and I flip, in playful delight,
Each pocket holds wonders, a comical sight.
In this quirky abode, joy overflows,
Packed with memories only my heart knows.

The Embrace of Embellishments

Sparking sequins, an outfit's foe,
Clashing colors, but on the go!
A mirror hides a smirk behind,
Reflecting chaos, so well-defined.

I've got charms, and yes, they jingle,
Like a fool, a smile will swindle.
My fringes dance, as if they're alive,
Wonky buttons help me thrive!

A sassy scarf, it's quite the scene,
Entwined with oddities, colorful sheen.
Every stitch, a tale we weave,
What's inside? A space to believe!

With each flair and every twist,
My life's a comedy, none can resist.
So here's to the embellishments bold,
In this wild embrace, laughter unfolds.

Heartbeat in Hand

In the palm, what secrets dwell?
A cracked phone, but all is swell.
A fuzzy keychain, cute as pie,
Wiry hopes, like dreams, fly high.

Mixing change with cherished sighs,
Fortunes told through odd-shaped fries.
A packet of gum, I'll share with cheer,
And laughter bound with each new year.

A spare key to the heart of a friend,
When life gets tough, it's a perfect blend.
My tiny vault holds greater wealth,
In beat and pulse, there's hidden health.

So I carry my treasures, light on my toes,
In each little pocket, love freely flows.
A heartbeat cradled, a rhythm divine,
With joy and jest in the grand design.

Pocketfuls of Promise

What lies within this tattered seam?
Lollipops and a forgotten dream.
A ticket stub from a show gone wild,
Reminds me of laughter, mischief compiled.

Quirky notes passed, they make me grin,
Each paper gives a new tale to spin.
The promise of fun in every fold,
Here's to the stories yet to be told.

Mismatched socks and a rubber band,
Hold tight to hopes that life is grand.
I pull out confetti, left from a party,
With every laugh, it's never too hearty.

So here's to the pockets, the light that they bring,
With every trinket, a note to sing.
In this treasure trove, joy's the key,
A pocketful of promise, just wait and see!

Stitched Secrets of the Soul

In pockets deep, I hide my dreams,
With zippers that squeak, and quirky seams.
A lost sock finds its rightful throne,
Among crumpled hopes, it's never alone.

The purse holds whispers of days gone by,
With lipstick stories that make me sigh.
A keychain of laughter, a trinket or two,
An odd assortment that speaks of you.

Buttoned up wishes and receipts galore,
Some are treasures, while others are more.
A snack from last week, it's still in the mix,
All stitched together in a fabric fix.

With each twist and turn, I wrangle the loot,
One wild journey from change to a boot.
Humor's woven in threads of delight,
My handbag's a circus, oh what a sight!

Unzipped Feelings

My bag's like a diary with secrets confined,
A crinkled note left by someone unkind.
Flirting with chaos, the chaos of cash,
A receipt for a lunch that was more of a bash.

Popcorn and gum stuck beneath the lining,
A search for the lipstick? What perfect timing!
Crammed with my daydreams, half-baked schemes,
An unzipped feeling of laughter and memes.

My wallet a fortress where hopes are stored,
Among the loose change and a tooth that's ignored.
When life gets sticky, I rummage around,
For giggles and glitter that can always be found.

An unexpected find, a treasure or two,
A snapshot of joy that reminds me of you.
So here's to the bag, with its quirky appeal,
Unzipped feelings make life all the more real!

A Satchel of Sentiments

This satchel of mine, such a curious beast,
Houses my joys, and a bit of my least.
Crusty old snacks and some coins that don't jingle,
In a heartbeat, my heart starts to mingle.

It's bursting with hugs and maybe a tear,
A candy receipt from last Christmas, so dear.
A half-chewed pencil and memories leaked,
In the folds of my bag, my inner child peeked.

With every forgotten piece, comes a smile,
From old concert tickets to candy gone wild.
An echo of laughter, a trace of the past,
These sentiments keep me rooted, steadfast.

So here's to the satchel where feelings entwine,
Each pocket a story, one of a kind.
I carry it proudly, my whimsical stash,
With a wink at the world, I make a big splash!

Tucked Away Treasures

Tucked in the corners, my treasures reside,
A crumpled up note from a crush I can't hide.
A button that once fell from a jacket I wore,
In a dance of nostalgia, can't help but adore.

With gumdrops and giggles, my stash is so bright,
Each item sings stories by day and by night.
A tiny mascara that's lost all its art,
Yet carries the essence of love from the start.

Hidden away, there's a sprinkle of flair,
A feather, a napkin, a sweet little dare.
A traveler's heart in the fabric I weave,
These tucked away dreams make it hard to believe.

So here's to the treasures wrapped in delight,
From odd little gadgets to things just right.
In pockets and folds, let laughter ignite,
My life's quirky handbag, such a marvelous sight!

Unraveled Threads

In the depths of a purse, lies a mess,
Coins and gum, oh what a distress!
Lipstick tubes jostle for space,
While old receipts sprint in a race.

Crumpled notes from a date long gone,
Once sweet, now just an odd yawn.
A forgotten snack stuck in a seam,
What was once fresh, now lives in a dream.

Lurking in corners, a rare find awaits,
A lost gift card, getting second rates.
It's a treasure hunt, a comedy play,
Each dive in brings laughter our way.

Yet amidst the chaos, a heart finds cheer,
For within these walls, loved moments appear.
A saga untold in the grab and go,
A quirky dance in a bag's flow.

Woven Stories

Threads of laughter, stitched with care,
In pockets and pouches, stories laid bare.
A cheeky note, spilled gumdrops bright,
Each woven tale holds a funny bite.

Here's a lipstick, vintage from '99,
Its color's a mystery, was it once fine?
Matching lipstick and a sock on the run,
A true fashion statement, just for fun!

Keys jingle loud like a circus bell,
Every jostle feels like a hard sell.
Yet in this chaos, a friendship blooms,
Like mismatched socks, it effortlessly zooms.

Every pocket holds a giggle or grin,
In this handbag quest, who knows where it's been?
A heart stitched together with joy and jest,
In every layer, life's little quest.

The Fabric of Connection

Fabric woven with threads of delight,
In zippers and pouches, laughter takes flight.
A lost ticket for a movie so grand,
Packed snugly away, oh where did it land?

Memories tangled in tangled floss,
Sharing secrets of dimes and gloss.
Spare change chimes in a melodious ring,
As the fabric of life unveils its string.

Buttons from shirts that once were so fine,
Mixed with candy wrappers, aged like wine.
A pin from journeys that went off the chart,
Each piece crafted within this art.

Yet here connections are made with flair,
In laughter's embrace, no burden to bear.
Every twist in this fabric profound,
Shows just how joy in chaos is found.

Broken Zippers and Mended Hearts

Zippers so stubborn, won't budge a bit,
Each tangle and fuss, we refuse to admit.
A purse like a puzzle, where should it go?
It's a test for the heart, oh what a show!

Each broken clasp tells a tale of woe,
Yet inside, sweet moments begin to flow.
A snack found a home, keeps memories tight,
As laughter explodes in the soft moonlight.

Mended corners with colorful threads,
Signal of journeys like those we have led.
Through quirky repairs, our hearts beat fast,
These clever solutions, forever will last.

So let's embrace this handbag of cheer,
With broken zippers, let's draw near.
For even in flaws, connections ignite,
Making every stumble feel so very right.

A Mosaic of Moments

A mosaic of treasures crammed in so snug,
Spatulas, fortunes, and a squishy bug.
A collection of moments, each quirky and bright,
In this patchwork of chaos, humor takes flight.

Forgotten crumbs mingle with old gum bits,
A time capsule lives where each memory sits.
An umbrella from summer, now lost in the fray,
Turns into stories of splashy ballet.

Every button and token, a laugh to be shared,
Each piece in the puzzle shows someone cared.
With every zip forward, every clutch and pull,
Discovering joy sure makes the heart full.

In this handbag's embrace, life's mosaics align,
Where laughter and memories effortlessly shine.
Each moment a stitch in the fabric we wear,
Crafting a journey beyond compare.

The Cloak of Comfort

In pockets deep, my treasures lie,
A snack or two, oh me, oh my!
Worn like armor through the fray,
I march on, come what may.

Oh what fun this cloak can bring,
With mismatched keys and a silly ring!
It holds the weight of dreams and snacks,
My quirky life in colorful packs.

When I'm lost, it offers cheer,
My trusty sidekick, always near.
With every zip and every flap,
It's a hug in disguise, or a cozy nap!

So here I am, in style, I stride,
With my fluffy friend by my side.
Let laughter echo, let worries slide,
In this bright world, I'm filled with pride.

Unraveled Secrets

What secrets hide within my bag?
A sock, a pen, a mischievous rag.
Each little item tells a tale,
Of shopping trips and epic fails.

There's gum from May and coins from June,
A half-eaten pie, a lonely spoon.
Beneath the chaos, treasures lurk,
Like a love letter or a goofy smirk.

The jumbled mess has magic too,
Disguised as cab fare or a shoe.
With every find, a grin I wear,
Oh, what stories live in there!

So rummage through, you just might find,
A silly hat or a piece of mind.
Each tangled thread a joy to share,
A patchwork life, if you dare!

The Essence of Travel

Packed and ready with dreams untold,
My bag hums softly, a pouch of gold.
From city streets to sandy shores,
It carries laughter, adventures galore.

It knows the taste of sunset skies,
The whir of planes and the funny highs.
A souvenir, a coffee cup,
With memories rich, I fill it up.

Oh how it swells with tales so grand,
A jumping map from hands to hand.
No room for doubt, just fun in store,
Every trip counts, who could ask for more?

So come along, let's pack some fun,
With a splash of colors, we'll stun and run.
The world awaits, it's our playground,
In this vibrant bag, life's joys are found!

Handle with Care

Oh please be gentle, I must confess,
This playful purse is quite the mess.
With candy wrappers and a quirky note,
Every bump brings a new anecdote.

To carry joy, my heart's delight,
With every grab, it feels so right.
A little squish, a tiny spill,
But laughter makes it all a thrill!

Its zippers giggle, its straps embrace,
A cozy hug in the bustling race.
With every toss, there's magic here,
A hoot, a holler, let's make that clear!

So handle softly, give it love,
This bag's a treasure, sent from above.
Full of whimsy, let's set our flair,
In this jolly life, too fun to bear!

Holding Heartbeats

In the depths of my purse, treasures abound,
Old receipts, lost keys, laughter all around.
A crumpled love note, a crayon drawn heart,
Each little find plays a whimsical part.

I rummage and sift through this colorful knoll,
Finding sweet joy in the chaos, my soul.
A mint from last summer, a rogue gummy bear,
Life's tiny surprises, a fun little scare.

Lipstick and gum share a secretive laugh,
While my phone chimes in with a repetitive gaff.
Oh, the tales these pockets could tell if they spoke,
Of mishaps and memories hidden in some cloak.

So here's to my bag, a peculiar delight,
With treasures inside, all tucked in it tight.
With every small jingle, my heart takes a peep,
A whimsical vault, my secrets to keep.

Gossamer Dreams in Canvas

Twirling through life with a bag that can burst,
It hums with my whims, a magnificent thirst.
Strings of bright laughter spread wide like confetti,
As I search for my phone, unsure where it's set, be.

This fabric of nonsense is frayed at the seams,
But it's captured my essence, my giggles, my dreams.
A tea bag, a sock, and a stray fortune cookie,
Packed with such thoughts, it feels outright spooky.

With glittery charms that dangle and sway,
A curious gathering at the end of the day.
Red lipstick and coins, a suspect alliance,
Each item a joke, a childlike defiance.

Oh, canvas of chaos, swirl of delight,
You transport my heart into laughter each night.
Inside your embrace, I sway like a kite,
Living in echoes that sparkle so bright.

The Fabric of Friendship

Stitched in camaraderie, pockets of fun,
With patches of memories, all tangled in one.
A roll of film, and a silly old hat,
Each layer a story where laughter is at.

From coffee spills shared to late-night confessions,
We've tucked all our secrets in playful sessions.
Frayed edges and colors that dance in the light,
Every tear in the fabric a moment so bright.

Like quirky old quilts of laughter and tears,
Our bags tell of journeys through giggles and cheers.
Together we wander with flair and with grace,
This fabric of friendship, the silliest place.

So here's to the stitches that weave us as friends,
And all the absurdities that laughter extends.
With colors so bright, we embrace the unknown,
This fabric of friendship, our laughter has sewn.

Clutches of Compassion

In the chaos of life, a clutch pops to play,
Capsized by kindness in a humorous way.
With pockets of joy tucked amidst all the stuff,
It carries the weight of life's giggles enough.

A tissue from drama, a snack for a smile,
It holds onto moments, each joyful mile.
A tiny pink teddy, a note for a friend,
In clutches of comfort, our hearts can transcend.

With flair and with laughter, it bounces around,
A bag bold enough to lift spirits unbound.
From playful remarks to compassion displayed,
Each zipper can hold what the heart has conveyed.

So raise up your clutches and giggle along,
Where kindness and humor weave one happy song.
With every small swipe, we remember our part,
For these clutches of comfort, they're treasures of heart.

www.ingramcontent.com/pod-product-compliance
Lightning Source LLC
Chambersburg PA
CBHW070002300426
43661CB00141B/142

* 9 7 8 1 8 0 5 8 6 0 2 8 0 *